Yellow Umbrella Books are published by Capstone Press
151 Good Counsel Drive, P.O. Box 669, Mankato, Minnesota 56002
www.capstonepress.com

Library of Congress Cataloging-in-Publication Data
Cipriano, Jeri S.
　It's time! / by Jeri Cipriano.
　p. cm.
　Summary: Photographs and simple text present some of the many different ways
to measure time.
　ISBN 0-7368-2916-4 (hardcover)—ISBN 0-7368-2875-3 (softcover)
　1. Time—Juvenile literature. [1. Time. 2. Time measurements.] I. Title.
QB209.5.C57 2004
529—dc22
　　　　　　　　　　　　　　　　　　　　　　　2003007744

Editorial Credits

Editorial Director: Mary Lindeen
Editor: Jennifer VanVoorst
Photo Researchers: Scott Thoms, Wanda Winch
Developer: Raindrop Publishing

Photo Credits

It's Time

by Jeri Cipriano

Consultants: David Olson, Director of Undergraduate Studies, and Tamara Olson, PhD, Associate Professor, Department of Mathematical Sciences, Michigan Technological University

Yellow Umbrella Books

an imprint of Capstone Press
Mankato, Minnesota

Everything you do takes time.
Some things take a long time.

It takes a long time to grow tall.

Some things take a short time.
It takes a short time to kick
a ball.

We can measure time. We can
measure it in seconds. It takes
about a second to raise your hand.

It takes about a second
to give a kiss.

We can measure time in
minutes. It takes about a
minute to tie your shoes.

We can measure time in hours.
It takes about an hour to play
a game.

It takes about an hour to bake cookies.

Clocks show time in hours
and minutes.

Do you know what time it is?

We can also measure time in days. Every day has a beginning and an end.

What is your favorite time
of day?

We can measure time in weeks.
There are seven days in a week.

We can measure time in
months. We celebrate different
holidays in different months.

We can also measure time in years. How many years old are you?

Words to Know/Index

Word Count: 175
Early-Intervention Level: 12